CONTENTS

KT-132-068

WHAT IS THE EQUATOR?

The equator is an imaginary line around the middle of the Earth. It is the same distance from the **North Pole** and the **South Pole**.

This painted red line shows the path of the equator.

EQUATOR
LATITUDE: 0°- 0'- 0"
LONG. OCC. 78°- 27'- 8"

FACT CAT

EQUATOR

Izzi Howell

WAYLAND

FACT CAT

Get your paws on this fantastic new mega-series from Wayland!

Join our Fact Cat on a journey of fun learning about every subject under the sun!

Published in paperback in 2016 by Wayland
Copyright © Wayland 2016

ISBN: 978 0 7502 9021 0
Library ebook ISBN: 978 0 7502 9020 3
Dewey Number: 910.9'13-dc23
10 9 8 7 6 5 4 3 2 1

MIX
Paper from
responsible sources
FSC® C104740

Wayland
An imprint of Hachette Children's Group
Part of Hodder & Stoughton
Carmelite House
50 Victoria Embankment
London EC4Y 0DZ

An Hachette UK Company
www.hachette.co.uk
www.hachettechildrens.co.uk

A catalogue for this title is available from
the British Library
Printed and bound in China

Produced for Wayland by
White-Thomson Publishing Ltd
www.wtpub.co.uk

Editor: Izzi Howell
Design: Rocket Design (East Anglia) Ltd
Fact Cat illustrations: Shutterstock/Julien Troneur
Other illustrations: Stefan Chabluk
Consultant: Kate Ruttle

Picture and illustration credits:
Corbis: Magali Delporte/Design Pics 19; iStock: Villamilk 11; Shutterstock: Pablo Hidalgo - Fotos593 cover and 18, Pal Teravagimov title page, Jennifer Stone 4, Ramona Heim 6, Monkey Business Images 7b, West Coast Scapes 8, Conny Sjostrom 9, Worldpics 10, Evdokim Eremenko 14, Pecold 15, Elena Mirage 16, tristan tan 17, apple2499 20; Stefan Chabluk 5, Thinkstock: Don Arnold 7t, MagicColors 12, balasclick 13, EvaKaufman 21.

Every effort has been made to clear copyright. Should there be any inadvertent omission, please apply to the publisher for rectification.

The author, Izzi Howell, is a writer and editor specialising in children's educational publishing.

The consultant, Kate Ruttle, is a literacy expert and SENCO, and teaches in Suffolk.

FACT CAT FACT

There is a question for you to answer on each spread in this book. You can check your answers on page 24.

The equator passes through four **continents** – Africa, Asia, South America and Australasia and Oceania. The line of the equator does not go through Antarctica, Europe or North America.

The equator goes through three of the Earth's five oceans – the Pacific Ocean, the Atlantic Ocean and the Indian Ocean.

Arctic Ocean

North America

Europe

Asia

Atlantic Ocean

Pacific Ocean

Africa

equator

South America

Pacific Ocean

Indian Ocean

Australasia and Oceania

Southern O...

FACT CAT FACT

The equator is at the widest part of the Earth. Find out the distance around the Earth at the equator.

THE NORTHERN AND SOUTHERN HEMISPHERES

The equator splits the Earth into two parts – the northern hemisphere and the southern hemisphere.

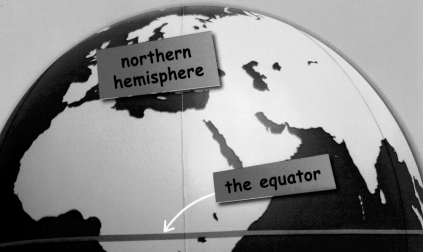

northern hemisphere

the equator

southern hemisphere

FACT CAT FACT

The word hemisphere means half of a sphere. A sphere is a 3D circle, such as the Earth, or a football.

The continent of Africa is in both hemispheres. Find out the name of an African country in the northern hemisphere.

In the northern hemisphere, winter lasts from December to March and summer lasts from June to September. In the southern hemisphere, the seasons are the other way round.

In the southern hemisphere, it is summer in December. These people are celebrating Christmas on the beach!

In the northern hemisphere, December is a winter month. This family is choosing their Christmas tree, dressed in warm clothes.

DAY AND NIGHT

At the equator, day and night are the same length all year long. Both day and night last for around 12 hours.

The sun rises and sets at the same time every day in Maldives. This is because it lies very close to the equator. Find out which ocean the Maldive islands are in.

FACT CAT FACT

Sunrises and sunsets at the equator only take a few minutes. This is much faster than anywhere else on Earth.

In the northern and southern hemispheres, the length of day and night changes throughout the year. In summer, days are longer and nights are shorter, while in winter, it's the other way round.

These people in Sweden are celebrating Midsummer, the day with the most hours of daylight in a year. In the northern hemisphere, this day is at the end of June.

WEATHER

Most places on the equator have warm weather all year round. Some areas on the equator, such as Indonesia, have two seasons – wet and dry. The wet season lasts for most of the year.

This Indonesian farmer is **harvesting** rice. Rice needs a lot of water to grow, so the wet season is very important for farmers.

Mountains on the equator have cold weather. This is because of their height – the higher the land, the colder the temperature.

Volcán Cayambe

Volcán Cayambe is a volcano that lies on the equator in South America. Its **peak** is so high that it is covered in snow all year round.

FACT CAT FACT

Volcán Cayambe hasn't **erupted** since 1786. Scientists don't think that it will erupt again soon. Find out which country Volcán Cayambe is in.

HABITATS

Rainforests grow in warm, wet areas along the equator, in countries such as Brazil. They are home to many different types of plants and animals.

These macaw parrots live in the Amazon Rainforest, the biggest in the world. The equator passes through the north of this rainforest.

In east Africa, there are savannahs close to the equator. A savannah is a grassy, dry **habitat** without many trees.

These giraffes live in the savannahs of the Serengeti **national park**. The Serengeti national park is found in northeast Tanzania.

FACT CAT FACT

More than 3,000 lions live in the Serengeti. Find out the name for a group of lions.

AFRICA

The equator passes through seven African countries, from Somalia on the east **coast** to Gabon on the west coast. In east Africa, it goes through Lake Victoria, the biggest lake on the continent.

These African buffaloes are cooling down in the waters of Lake Victoria. Find out which three countries Lake Victoria is in.

FACT CAT FACT

One African country on the equator isn't connected to **mainland** Africa by land. São Tomé and Príncipe is an island in the Atlantic Ocean but we still think of it as a part of Africa.

Some large African cities are near the equator. In Uganda, the equator is only 30 km to the south of its **capital** city, Kampala.

This monument marks the path of the equator through Uganda. People like to have their photo taken here.

ASIA

Only two Asian countries, Indonesia and Maldives, lie on the equator. Indonesia is made up of thousands of islands but the equator only passes through eight of them. These eight islands include Sumatra and Borneo.

This bridge is in Bukittinggi, a Sumatran city on the equator.

Borneo is home to the **endangered** Bornean orangutan. Find another endangered animal that lives in Borneo.

Borneo is the third-largest island in the world. The equator passes through its biggest city, Samarinda. In other parts of the island, thick **tropical** rainforests grow along the equator.

FACT CAT FACT

More than 1,000 different types of insects can be found in just one Dipterocarp tree in the rainforests of Borneo.

SOUTH AMERICA

ECUADOR   0°· 0'· 0" LAT.

The equator goes through three countries in the north of South America: Brazil, Colombia and Ecuador. Ecuador is even named after the equator – 'ecuador' means equator in Spanish.

In Ecuador, the Mitad del Mundo monument marks the line of the equator. Find out the capital city of Ecuador.

In Colombia, the tall Andes mountains are near the equator. The Andes make up the longest mountain range in the world. They stretch along the entire west coast of South America.

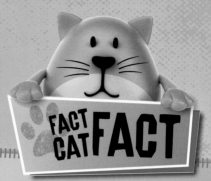

FACT CAT FACT

In Macapá, a town in Brazil, the equator passes through the middle of a football stadium. One half of the pitch is in the southern hemisphere, and the other half is in the northern hemisphere!

These girls are taking part in a festival in Bogotá, the capital of Colombia. Bogotá is high in the Andes mountains.

AUSTRALASIA AND OCEANIA

Nauru and Kiribati are the only countries in Australasia and Oceania that are close to the equator. Both are small islands in the Pacific Ocean.

Pandan trees grow in Nauru, where the weather is hot and **humid**. Pandan leaves can be made into **fabric**. Find out if humans can eat Pandan fruit.

The country of Kiribati is made up of 33 islands on either side of the equator. The islands are **surrounded** by **coral reefs** and warm tropical water.

FACT CAT FACT

The islands that make up Kiribati are spread far apart. They cover an area of more than 3.5 million square kilometres – bigger than the country of India! The distance between some islands is over 3,000 kilometres.

Try to answer the questions below. Look back through the book to help you. Check your answers on page 24.

1 Which of these continents does the equator pass through?

a) Europe

b) Asia

c) Antarctica

2 Day and night are the same length of time at the equator. True or not true?

a) true

b) not true

3 Most places along the equator have cold weather. True or not true?

a) true

b) not true

4 How many African countries does the equator pass through?

a) Four

b) Six

c) Seven

5 Which South American country is named after the equator?

a) Bolivia

b) Ecuador

c) Brazil

6 Nauru and Kiribati are in the Atlantic Ocean. True or not true?

a) true

b) not true

GLOSSARY

capital the city where a country's government meet

coast the area where the land meets the ocean

continent one of the seven main areas of land on Earth, such as Africa or North America

coral reef a tropical sea habitat made from coral

cruise a holiday on a boat that sails to different places

endangered an animal or plant is endangered when there are only very few of its kind left in the world

erupt when smoke and lava come out of a volcano

fabric material that clothes are made from

habitat the area where a plant or an animal lives

harvest to pick plants and fruit when they are ready to eat

humid hot and wet weather

mainland the main part of a country or a continent, not including the islands around it

national park an area of land that is protected

North Pole the northernmost point on Earth

peak the top of a mountain

South Pole the southernmost point on Earth

surround to be around something

tourist someone who visits a place on holiday but does not live there

tropical hot and wet

INDEX

ANSWERS

Pages 5-20

Page 5: 40,075 kilometres

Page 6: Some countries include Algeria, Chad and Egypt

Page 7: The Indian Ocean

Page 11: Ecuador

Page 13: a pride

Page 14: Uganda, Kenya and Tanzania

Page 17: Some animals include Borneo pygmy elephants and the proboscis monkey

Page 18: Quito

Page 20: Yes, pandan fruit is edible

Quiz answers

1 b) Asia

2 a) true

3 b) not true – most places have warm weather

4 c) seven

5 b) Ecuador

6 b) not true – they are in the Pacific Ocean